D1556028

First published in Great Britain in 1979 by
Ward Lock Limited, 116 Baker Street,
London W1M 2BB, a Pentos Company.

Designed and produced for Ward Lock Limited by
Asset Publishing Limited, 83A Queen Street,
Maidenhead, Berkshire SL6 1LR

Copyright© 1979 Asset Publishing Limited
All rights reserved. No part of this publication may
be reproduced, stored in a retrieval system, or
transmitted, in any form or by any means, electronic,
mechanical, photocopying, recording or otherwise, without
the prior permission of the Copyright owners.

ISBN 0 7063 5722 1

Printed in Italy

ORIGINS AND BREEDS

Sally Gordon

Photographs by Sally Anne Thompson

Ward Lock Limited · London

Contents

Introduction

Just as there are many different races and nationalities of people and various breeds of dogs and cats, so there are more than 200 types of horses and ponies living in the world today. Many are native to a particular place; that is they have been living there for thousands and thousands of years, breeding and existing naturally and unchanged over the centuries. The Icelandic Pony, the Arab and the pony breeds of the British Isles are just a few examples of these native breeds. Other breeds have been 'created' by man, who, as he learnt more about animal husbandry and how to control selective breeding among horses, crossed different breeds with one another to produce an animal that would suit some particular and specific purpose he had in mind. The greatest and most famous of all such 'created' breeds is the Thoroughbred, produced by man to satisfy his desire to race horses against one another.

In addition to the breeds, some horses, such as Palominos, Pintos and Appaloosas, are identified and classified according to their coat coloration or markings. Other horses are termed by the specific purpose for which they have been bred—such as a hunter or polo pony, a show pony or a show jumper.

In the following pages, we trace the evolution of the horse, see how the various breeds and types emerged and developed, and describe the main characteristics of some of the breeds. In addition, there is an explanation of the different colours and markings by which all horses and ponies—whatever their breed or type—may be described.

The Origin of the Horse

The story of the horse began some 60 million years ago in that period of pre-history known as the Eocene. At this stage in the earth's development, the land masses and mountain ranges had begun to form and plant life and animals had long emerged from the sea to prove themselves capable of a land-based existence.

It is unlikely that any of us would recognize the first ancestor of early horses as a relative of the equines we know today. Known as Hyracotherium, Eohippus and the 'Dawn Horse', it was only about 37cm (15ins) high and had a concave-arched back. The main difference from today's horses was that this animal possessed toes—three on its hind feet and four on the front feet. Adapted to a browsing diet of succulent leaves that grew above its head, its teeth were also very different from those of the modern grazing animal.

The early 'horse' was to undergo a number of distinct evolutionary changes during the geological periods that followed. Unable to adapt sufficiently itself to live successfully in its changing surroundings, Eohippus died out about 40 million years ago and was replaced by Orohippus and also Epihippus. Standing a little taller than their predecessor, these animals had teeth which had become a little flatter, reflecting a change in their diet.

Up until this time, these equine ancestors frequented parts of the world we would now define as North America and Europe. They appear to have been wiped out of Europe by the dramatic floods of the Oligocene period (40 to 25 million BC). Epihippus lived on in North America and evolved into Mesohippus, still during the Oligocene period. This creature showed still more definite adaptations to cope with its changing environment, where the jungles had been washed away to leave wide open areas of grassy plains. If the horse's ancestors were to survive now, they had to be grazers rather than browsers. Also, being non-aggressive, non-hunting her-

Below: A mare and foal of the wild horse, Equus Caballus. Some representatives of this breed may still be found roaming wild in small herds in parts of Mongolia. Owing to the vastness of the area and the widely differing characteristics of the terrain, several localized variations in the breed have developed.

bivores, they had to be able to run fast if they were going to escape the carnivorous predators of the plains. Mesohippus had three toes on each foot and a straighter back, both of which would have contributed to a greater turn of speed than its arch-backed, multi-toed ancestors.

Towards the Oligocene period, Miohippus evolved from Mesohippus. The lateral toes on its fore and hind feet no longer came into contact with the ground, rendering them quite useless. It was followed by Parahippus, which appeared during the Miocene period (25 to 10 million BC) and then Mercyhippus. Parahippus' skeletal stucture has indications of the formation of withers, which was a new development and these became even more pronounced in Mercyhippus. The teeth of Mercyhippus, too, were almost identical to those of today's horses. Furthermore, it is said to have had a dun-coloured coat and a heavy head, making it apparently very similar in appearance to some of the more 'primitive' types of native pony extant today.

In the Pliocene period that followed the Miocene, the first ancestor to be truly recognizable as a 'horse' evolved. This was Pliohippus, the first mono-

dactyl or one-hoofed animal to exist. It stood about three times as tall as Eohippus and is generally considered to be the true ancestor of our modern horse.

Whilst the remains of Pliohippus have been found extensively in North and Central America, it is known that its direct descendants, if not it too, migrated to Eurasia via the land bridges that were still in existence. It thus began to perpetuate the race in these areas again. Pliohippus extended into the Pleistocene period which saw the birth of Equus Caballus, the progenitor

Above: It seems likely that horses were broken to be used in harness before saddles were placed on their backs.

Left: Equus Caballus *seen here in their sleek coats of the summer.*

of all animals known as horses today. Indeed many people consider Equus Caballus to be one and the same as Equus Przewalskii, a primitive pony still living in Mongolia, but only discovered there at the end of last century by a Russian explorer, after whom it is named. The two animals (Equus Caballus and Equus Przewalskii) certainly bear a striking resemblance to one another.

Equus Caballus was thought to have originated in North America, there-after spreading quickly through South America and—as it was unimpeded by oceans—across to Europe and Asia. For reasons that have never been satisfactorily explained, it disappeared algether from the Americas towards the end of the Pleistocene period some 10,000 years ago, but lived on in Eurasia. Horses were absent altogether from North and South America until they were re-introduced there by Cortez and his Spanish conquistadores in the early sixteenth century.

Below: A reconstruction of the extinct European wild horse, Tarpan.

The Development of Types: Emergence of Breeds

It is after the coming of Equus Caballus that the theories and opinions about the development of the equine race diverge. Some say all types of modern horse developed from one animal that was similar to, if not actually, Equus Przewalskii. Others claim that the huge variety of types and breeds in existence today could not have developed from just this one creature and a varying number of wild horse types must be responsible. The number of these varies between two and six, with four perhaps being the most popularly supported number. These are generally categorized as Types 1, 2, 3 and 4.

Type 1 was of pony size (see page 16) and said to inhabit north-western Europe. It stood about 12.2 h.h. and was generally brown or dark bay in colour. Its straight facial profile, small ears, meanly-coloured nose and under belly, and thick mane and tail are reminiscent of the Exmoor pony (see page 54), which it closely resembles.

Type 2, on the other hand, more closely resembles Przewalski's Horse, It grew a little taller than Type 1 and was generally heavier-boned. It had a coarse head and a dun-coloured coat with black mane (which was brush-like and scrubby and stood erect from the crest), black tail and lower legs and a black dorsal strip running down its back. This colouring, together with bar (slightly stripey) markings on the top part of the legs, when seen today, are considered to be indicative of an ancient ancestry. This pony inhabited the treeless tundra of northern Eurasia.

Type 3 was found in central Asia, extending westwards as far as Spain. Considerably taller than Types 1 and 2, it could be as much as 15 h.h. and seems to have possessed varying coat colours, ranging from golden dun through to black. Of poor and weak conformation, it had a large, ugly head with a pronounced Roman nose (see page 18) and long ears, a long, straight, weak neck, flat sides and a markedly sloping croup. Its coat was thin and its mane and tail were sparse and lanky.

Type 4 was an inhabitant of central Asia and although definitely only of pony height, standing some 12 h.h., it apparently more closely resembled a miniature horse in appearance. It was fine-boned, with a distinctively Arab-type head—concave profile, broad forehead between the eyes and small ears. It had a fine coat, which appears to have been grey, bay or chestnut in colour, and a silky-haired mane and tail, the latter of which was set unusually high—another characteristic feature of the Arab. In addition it had a short back, level croup and slender legs.

Left: Przewalski's Horses graze quietly. Possibly the most primitive of all ponies in the world, Equus Przewalskii *at one time inhabited the same area as* Equus Caballus. *A few may still be found in this region, but more will be seen in the major zoos of the world.*

The natural territories of these four types overlapped to some extent, so that it is reasonable to assume that some intermingling and cross-breeding took place. Types 1 and 2 were neighbours and are thought to be responsible in large measure for most of the native ponies found in northern Europe. Types 2 and 3 would not have come into contact with one another all that frequently during the normal course of their lives. It is possible, though, that when man realized the type of offspring that resulted from such a cross, he engineered more frequent meetings between the two.

For, given favourable conditions of adequate food and shelter against cold, a taller and heavier animal of draught type was produced, and this would have been of immense value to man. Crosses between types 3 and 4 also produced a useful animal, rather lighter in build and believed to be the progenitor of all the modern light horse breeds.

Selective breeding by man, in which he works actively to produce horses of great beauty or speed, with kind, amenable temperaments or great en-

durance. strength and stamina is, in evolutionary terms, a comparatively recent development. Man has undoubtedly used horses since he first appeared on earth amongst them, prob-

Above: An elaborate portrayal of a mediaeval battle. Note the heavy build of the horses (necessary to carry the great weight of the armoured knights) and the armour some are wearing.

Left: A drawing by the famous German painter and engraver, Albert Dürer, of the Great Horse of the Middle Ages. Dürer lived from 1471–1528.

ably first as meat and very soon thereafter to carry him across the plains, as he realized the advantage this gave him in catching other animals. Later he realized, too, that he could harness the horse to primitive carriages, chariots or carts, thereby transporting his goods and chattels as well as himself from place to place considerably more easily than if he had to go on foot.

For centuries, horses as they existed in their wild state would have satisfied man's requirements and although lack of knowledge, ability and resources probably prevented any attempt at selective breeding, equally there was little need of it. Thus horses would have bred naturally and would themselves have been the results of 'natural' selective breeding. This inevitably leads to the 'survival of the fittest', that is, those most suited to survive the conditions of the immediate environment. This makes less for beautiful horses of good conformation and friendly temperament, than for those that are hardy and cunning, able perhaps to exist on poor sparse grazing and possessing the wit to outsmart others in getting what little food there is!

Early generations of 'horse breeders', capable though they undoubtedly were

Below: Horse used by the Cavaliers, from the painting by Van Dyck.

of handling their horses or ponies, probably had little control over the breeding. In very early times, the horses they caught would anyway have been the weaker specimens—the unsound or the stupid—the faster, clever animals obviously being the ones that could evade capture. Wild stallions would come off the plains to cover these 'domestic' mares. However, such a state of affairs does not appear to have lasted for too long, and primitive man was certainly controlling selective breeding of horses to a limited extent.

Successive centuries, or in some cases, generations, brought differences in the demands and needs placed by man on his horse. Early requirements would be for an animal that could carry weights—thus the development of the pack horse. From there there would have been a divergence, with a requirement for horses suitable for riding and for harness. Those areas where the greater requirement was for riding horses, for example, may not have possessed a suitable native type, so the business of horse trading between people and communities began. This led to far greater scope generally in the matter of breeding, and more and more

types of animal began to emerge in consequence.

During the Middle Ages, with the advent of heavy armour worn by the knights, there was a need for a strong riding horse capable of carrying the knights for considerable distances. The Great Horse of the Middle Ages was produced and was to survive for many centuries. Many of the heavy breeds known today are claimed to have descended from it. Clearly, it was not suitable for the knights' ladies to ride, so a lighter type of riding horse sprang up, too. In addition, there were carriage and pack horse types much in evidence.

So many factors have led to the emergence of varying breeds, it is impossible to cover more than a few of them in this book. As well as the greater knowledge of horsemastership —of feeding requirements and conditions most likely to produce better animals—man's other inventions wrought immense changes on horses too. Such things as the development of tack, particularly the stirrup, and subsequent changes brought about in styles and types of harness, combined with other factors like the building of hard roads, all had a great effect on the type of

Below: An Anglo-Arab. As with all Arabs, this horse is fast and fiery.

horse needed and produced.

Today, as you will see from the following pages, there are many different recognizable breeds and types, quite separate from one another, in existence in the world. A few of these, of which the Arab, the Andalusian and the Exmoor Pony would be examples, have their origins in antiquity and we are not even now completely certain when they first appeared. More breeds, however, are the result of selective breeding by man. These have all been developed in an effort to produce animals that would meet his specific requirements, or to keep perpetuating the characteristics he favoured. Selective breeding of the Arab, for example, which is known to have gone on longer than with any other type of breed, was rigorously controlled by the early desert Bedouins, to keep the line absolutely pure. It was not until later that the Arab was widely used in the development of other breeds. The greatest of all created breeds largely attributable to the Arab is the Thoroughbred (see page 24), an animal initially created purely for speed.

Horses and pones could at one stage be divided into 'hot' and 'cold-blooded'

types. The 'hot-blooded' types, of which the Arab is again the prime example, generally emanated from the warmer climatic areas and are finely built, fast-moving and somewhat fiery in temperament. The 'cold-bloods' come from the colder regions of the world and are rather heavier in build, more docile in temperament and slower and more deliberate in movement. Of course, these types have now been widely crossed and interbred so that many breeds today may be termed 'warm-bloods'.

Above: The picture clearly shows the beautiful head of the Arab.

Left: The Exmoor Pony has its origins dating. back to antiquity.

Identifying Horses and Ponies

The essential difference between a horse and a pony is size. Both animals are measured in 'hands'. A hand is 10cm (4ins) and the measurement is taken in a straight line from the ground to the point of the withers. Fractions of a hand are written as .1 (2.5cm: 1in), .2 (5cm: 2ins) etc. Ponies stand up to 14.2 hands high (commonly abbreviated to h.h.), and horses are any height over this.

A full description of any individual horse or pony will always include a definition of its coat colour, and very often, any distinguishing marks it may have, such as white markings on its face or legs. There are several different coat colours, all of which have special names and definitions. Colours are also referred to as solid—when the entire coat is basically the same colour; and broken—when there are patches of different colours on the body. In describing a coat colour, the word 'points' is often used—this embraces the mane, tail and lower part of the legs.

The coat colours are as follows:

Chestnut: a solid colour that varies from golden yellow to reddish brown. The points are usually the same colour as the rest of the coat, although the mane and tail may occasionally be lighter. Chestnut-coloured horses or ponies may be described as golden, light, bright, dark or liver, according to the shade. The colours are all as the name suggests —a liver chestnut being a more subdued muted shade, rather closer to brown than the usual chestnut.

Bay: this denotes a brown, solid coat with black points. Again bays may be described as dark, light or bright (or sometimes as mahogany or red). Dark and light are self-explanatory; bright refers to a bright, very reddish brown which often also has a black 'dorsal' stripe (a narrow stripe running from the withers, right down the spine to the top of the tail).

Brown: a solid brown coat colour with the same coloured points. This is usually a duller colour than bay. If a horse has a black coat, which tends to be brownish black in winter, with a brown muzzle and brown rims to the nostrils, it is also known as brown. Sometimes a horse is said to be *bay-brown*. This means it does not quite conform to either coat colour; its mane and tail may contain both brown and black hairs, for example.

Black: to be called black, the coat must be jet black all over in summer and winter, except for any permissable white markings (see next page).

Roan: this refers to bay, chestnut or black coats which are intermingled equally with white hairs (that is *not* patches, but the different coloured hairs mixing together evenly). Bay and chestnut and white are known as red or strawberry roans; black and white hairs mixed together make a blue roan.

Grey: varying shades of grey-coloured coat from a dark grey to almost pure white. Many grey horses are born black; in any event, all become lighter in shade each time they shed their winter coats. Grey coats nearly always contain a proportion of black hairs through the coat: if these are present in tufts, the coat colour is described as

Below: Even when the coat of a horse or pony is almost pure white, it is still known as grey. A very white coat is often an indication of old age as the coat tends to get lighter as the horse or pony matures.

Left: There are six recognized Appaloosa coat patterns; the one illustrated is called the blanket, which is considered to be the classic pattern. It comprises a dark forepart with a white blanket shape over the loin and hips (this can vary in size) spotted with dark round or egg-shaped spots.

Below: This Canadian horse has an extremely unusual coat colour. It could either be an extremely dark grey or a roan.

fleabitten grey. If they occur in circles, it is known as dappled grey.

Albino: this very rare colour is sometimes also referred to as pink grey, as the total lack of pigmentation in the skin makes it pink (most horses, even greys, generally have black skins except where pure white markings occur). Albinos have a pure white coat. The eyes are usually pale blue.

Cream: a cream-coloured coat, with points of the same colour. This, again, is generally the result of very little pigmentation in the skin. The eyes are usually light-coloured or pale blue.

Dun: a pale sandy or dark cream colour, usually with black points and a black dorsal stripe. If the coat has a greyish tinge, rather than a cream colour, it is known as a blue dun.

Palomino: a creamy, golden coat, with the mane and tail a lighter shade, often tending towards silver (see also page 20).

Piebald: this denotes a coat which features large irregular patches of white and black. The mane, tail and legs may be white or black or a similar irregular mixture of the two.

Skewbald: the same definition as piebald except it denotes irregular patches of white and any shade of brown, chestnut or bay. These two patterned coats are referred to collectively as 'Pinto' in the USA.

Left: Albino horses, such as this one, are extremely rare. The lack of skin pigmentation is apparent from the pink of the muzzle and also from the pinkish tinge to the skin behind the elbow. Note, too, the blue eyes surrounded by pink rims—this is further indication of albinism.

Spotted or Appaloosa: this is discussed in greater detail on page 21, but refers to a coat which is covered with small round or oval spots. In an Appaloosa, the basic coat colour is usually roan and the spots are black or chocolate coloured. They can be arranged in various recognized patterns. Some spotted horses have basically white coats with darker coloured spots.

Horses and ponies that live in a natural state out of doors change their coats in spring and autumn. There may be slight differences in shade between the resulting 'winter' and 'summer' coats, the winter coat is often a little darker and duller as it is thicker and woollier than the sleeker, smoother, finer hairs of the summer coat.

The other distinguishing features of a horse or pony are the white markings many of them have on their faces and legs.

Those on the face have various names according to their shape and size: a *blaze* is a broad white stripe stretching from the forehead to the muzzle. It can be varying widths—if it is very narrow, it becomes known as a *stripe*;

if it is so wide it extends over the forehead and eyes too, then it is referred to as a *white* face. A small white mark between the nostrils is known as a *snip*: a white mark on the forehead between the eyes is a *star*, which may be further defined as large or irregular (if it is very unsymmetrical).

White markings on the legs are referred to as *socks* if they extend upwards from the hoof over the fetlock joint and *stockings* if they reach up to the knee or hock. Higher than this and it would be described as a *white leg*; or if there is only a small amount of white, the actual part would be defined —such as a white coronet, fetlock, heel or pastern.

In addition, in describing a horse or pony, it is often said it has either a 'Roman nose' or a 'dished face'. A Roman nose refers to a convex profile to the face: a dished face usually denotes a concave profile. A Roman nose usually indicates some common or heavy horse type blood in the lineage, while a dished face is one of the distinguishing characteristics of the Arab and its descendants.

Opposite: A strikingly marked Pinto horse. This coat coloration is known also as a piebald. The animal pictured here displays an unusual amount of solid black; this is more usually interspersed with patches of white.

Opposite, inset: A beautifully coloured Palomino.

Horse and Pony Types

In addition to the individual breeds of horses and ponies, described on the following pages, there are a number of equines that are essentially 'types' rather than breeds. Among these are the 'coloured' horses such as Palominos and Pintos, and also those animals that have come to be recognized as being suited to a certain occupation or activity such as a hunter, a hack or show pony.

The Palomino

Palominos may be either horses or ponies — the characteristic feature being their golden-coloured coat and silvery-white mane and tail. To qualify for registration with the recognized Palomino societies, the coat colour must conform to shades 'three times lighter or darker than a newly-minted gold coin'. The coat must be of a uniform colour, with no lighter or darker patches and no white markings, except on the face and lower legs. Societies vary in the standards laid down for the mane and tail; some say it must be pure white, while others allow up to fifteen per cent of the hairs to be darker.

In some parts of the USA, the Palomino is considered as a breed, and efforts are being made in the breeding to produce a recognizable type as well as an acceptable coat colour. This is having the desirable effect of eliminating shortcomings in conformation, previously allowed to be perpetuated because of the emphasis placed on colour. Palominos are show and riding animals rather than 'work' horses.

Below: Another example of an Appaloosa. This one has the more unusual leopard markings, in which the base coat colour is white. Dark spots are distributed evenly over the entire body. The foal pictured here, incidentally, will not inherit its dam's markings, for leopard Appaloosas are born spotted.

The Albino

Almost all breeds of horse and pony could be Albino, as the name refers to the lack of pigmentation in the skin. This produces a pure white coat, with a skin that is pink (instead of the more usual black or brown) and very sensitive, and eyes that are a translucent pale blue colour, often with impaired sight. Albinos generally occur by accident rather than design, although there is an American Albino Horse Club which has long encouraged the breeding of pure Albinos. It has had considerable success in produing Albinos with less sensitive skins and darker eyes that are less prone to defect.

The Pinto

Pintos are traditionally associated with the American Indians of the 'Wild West'. The term refers to horses with piebald or skewbald coats (see page 21). There are two basic coat patterns—the Tobiano, which has a predominantly white coat and white legs, with large, coloured patches mainly on the head, neck, chest and flanks, and the Overo, which comprises a dark-coloured coat with patches of white usually on the middle part of the body—seldom across the back. The legs are dark. Pintos can be any shape or size, although they are generally of a recognized riding type, and are sometimes also known as Paint Horses. An association was formed in the early 60s, called the American Paint Horse Association, which is striving to establish a Western Stock type of horse with these coat colours. In order to do this, strict breeding regulations are imposed on those horses that are registered.

The Appaloosa

This is in fact a recognized breed, but as its distinguishing feature is its variously spotted coat, it is included here. Spotted horses are known from primitive cave drawings to have existed some 20,000 years ago, but the Appaloosa is descended from the Spanish horses taken to America by the Spanish conquistadores. Many of these found their way into the hands of the Indians, and it is the tribe known as the Nez Percé, who lived near the Palouse river in the north-west, who were responsible for developing this breed.

Of riding horse conformation and build, Appaloosas generally stand between 14 and 15.3 h.h. The coat is usually a roan colour and the spots are distributed in six recognized patterns— frost, leopard, marble, snowflake, and spotted and white blanket patterns. The names are self-explanatory—blanket marking indicates spots of various sizes and colour distributed over the hindquarters while the forehand is usually an unbroken colour; leopard is dark spots distributed all over a white, light grey or cream coat while snowflake is white, often irregularly shaped, spots on a darker coat. Frost and marble indicates speckles rather than clearly-defined spots.

Above top: The horse on the far left of the picture shows the basic pattern of a Tobiano Paint Horse.

Above: An American Paint Horse. The markings here are unusual in that the predominance of white in the coat would normally be accompanied by white legs.

The Hunter

The straightforward definition of this type of horse is, quite simply, one that is suited to foxhunting. Although the requirements vary a little according to the type of country in which it is to be hunted and the weight and ability of the rider, the hunter generally stands between 15 and 17 h.h., has good conformation and jumping ability, boldness, courage, an equable temperament, good manners and sufficient strength and stamina to carry his rider through a long and tiring day's hunting.

Show hunters, which never go near the hunting field, are also bred purely for the show ring. They are judged on conformation which must give an impression of substance and power, and performance, in which paces and action are very important. Hunter classes are divided into heavyweight, middleweights and lightweights (referring to the amount of weight they can carry), small and ladies. In addition, there are show classes for working hunters, where performance, which includes jumping, is more important than conformation. The most prized type of hunters are generally Irish Hunters (see page 26).

The Hack

Nowadays almost exclusively thought of as a show animal, the hack is essentially a riding horse—hence the expression 'to go for a hack'. At one stage there were two recognized types; those ridden by gentlemen to a meet of hounds (their precious hunters being ridden at

Below: A majestic hunter, plaited ready for the show ring. The strong shoulders, hindquarters and broad back indicate it would be well able to keep going through a hard day's hunting.

a more leisurely pace by the groom, to preserve them for the day's sport) and those, rather more elegant in type, ridden in fashionable parks by fashionable men and women.

Hacks are generally small Thoroughbred horses and are animals of quite outstanding beauty. Usually shown by ladies, for whom they make a perfect ride, they must not be more than 15.3 h.h. for the show ring and must have perfect conformation, graceful movement, elegant carriage and perfect manners.

The Cob
This again is a type, rather than a breed of horse, and denotes a heavy, stocky, sturdy sort of animal, usually with a good, honest head, a powerful neck, short back with deep girth and strong rounded hindquarters. It stands between 14.2 and 15.2 h.h. and usually has a hogged mane (clipped right off) which shows off its crested neck to best advantage. At one time, it was traditional to dock the tails of cobs too (i.e. cut off at the dock), but this cruel practice has been made illegal. Its conformation coupled with its usually kind, gentle temperament make the cob an ideal ride for elderly, heavy riders who want a pleasant, rather than a fiery ride.

In days gone by cobs, as well as being riding horses, were widely used in harness and were a familiar sight pulling tradesmen's vans in towns and cities. The lack of demand in this area has made good cobs quite hard to come by and they are mostly bred for the show ring now. Among the best known of all cobs is the Welsh Cob (Section D in the Welsh Stud Book), which is, of course, a recognized breed of horse.

The Show Pony
This is a type of animal that has been developed in the last few decades, mainly in Great Britain, for the show ring. It has generally been produced by crossing native-bred mares (very often Welsh Mountain Ponies) with small Thoroughbred and Arab stallions. The aim has been to produce a perfect pony for a child, and as such they are divided into three main categories—up to 12.2 h.h., 13.2 h.h., and 14.2 h.h. Conformation has to be as near faultless as possible, but as many show ponies can claim this, strong emphasis is placed on performance and manners in the judging.

Top: A magnificently built cob. It is thicker and stockier than the hunter.

Above: A prizewinning hack. The head is refined and elegant and the legs finely boned.

Left: Judges examine the conformation and general appearance of ponies shown in hand.

23

Horse Breeds of the British Isles

The Thoroughbred

The Thoroughbred is the most famous of all horse breeds in Great Britain and it rates as one of the most important and valuable breeds in the world today. Often referred to as the English Racehorse, it is to racing that it owes much of its origin. Charles II founded races at Newmarket, thus giving racing royal patronage where it had previously been frowned upon as a sport. This was sufficient to make the breeding of horses that could gallop faster, both respectable and systematic.

In the early eighteenth century, three Arab horses were brought to England and they became the progenitors of the Thoroughbred horse. Almost all pure Thoroughbreds today could be traced back to one or other, and often all three, of these horses. They were called Byerley Tuck, the Darley Arabian (who was an ancestor of the unbeaten racehorse, Eclipse) and the Godolphin Arabian. The horses were mated with carefully selected mares, many of which had Oriental blood in their veins, and others that had already proved themselves as worthy contestants on the racecourse. From them, the Thoroughbred as we know it evolved and today a horse can only be registered in the General Stud Book as pure Thoroughbred if its lineage can be traced, unbroken on both sides to others recorded in the register.

The average height of a Thoroughbred is between 15 and 17 h.h. and they may be black, brown, chestnut, bay or grey. Their conformation varies slightly according to whether they have been bred for racing or for some other purpose, such as a hunter or hack. In general, however, they have a refined, clean-boned head, with large bright eyes, a long, elegant, well-arched neck, sloping, well-muscled shoulders and a deep chest. The back is short and strong with a good depth of girth, while the legs will be slender and long with good bone. They have a lively springy action and are generally fast-moving at all paces.

The Cleveland Bay

This is the only native horse breed (as opposed to pony) found in Great Britain, apart from the heavy horses. It comes from the Cleveland district of north

Above: Cleveland Bays find great favour with the driving and coaching fraternity. They may be seen worldwide in use as ceremonial coach horses as well as in competitive driving.

Left: Thoroughbred mares out at grass. These beautiful horses are now bred in a number of countries and show slight variations in conformation and style according to regional preference.

Yorkshire and has been used for farm work, as a pack horse in the mines and as a haulage animal for two centuries. In recent times, it has been extensively crossed with Thoroughbred blood to produce a horse that is smaller and more refined than its ancestors. Now it is much sought after as a riding horse and is frequently seen in the hunting field as well as in show jumping and eventing competitions. It is also still popular as a coach and carriage horse, and is used particularly in competitive driving.

Cleveland Bays stand between 15.2 and 16.2 h.h. and, as their name suggests, are generally some shade of bay. They have a relatively large head, usually with a slight, convex profile or 'Roman nose' (see page 18). The neck is fairly long and strong and the shoulders sloping and muscular. The back is

longer than in many breeds, the girth is deep and the hindquarters are strong and powerful. The legs tend to be a little on the short side, but they have hard, clean bone. Cleveland Bays are renowned for their intelligence, kindness and great stamina. Late to mature, they live long and are usually extremely fertile.

The Hackney
The showy Hackney is extremely popular with spectators at competitive events. These flamboyant horses, with their distinctive, spectacular, high-stepping knee action have been used as trotting horses by the people of East Anglia for several centuries. Although the Hackney as we now recognize it was developed from an extinct breed called

the Norfolk Roadster which was crossed with Arab and Thoroughbred stock, trotting horses known as Hackneys were in existence before the 'birth' of the Thoroughbred (this took place in the eighteenth century).

The Hackney is essentially a harness and show animal. Standing between 14.3 and 16 h.h., it has a small elegant head, carried high on a long, muscled neck. Its body is extremely compact, its legs short, strong and straight and its tail is set and carried high. Its proud but graceful appearance, coupled with its explosive, yet controlled, distinctive paces and fiery personality, make it a constant joy to watch. The most common coat colours are chestnut, dark brown or bay, often with lots of white markings.

Above: A beautiful example of a Hackney Pony bred in the United States of America. Note the extremely erect head and tail carriage (the tail is docked in many instances to achieve this — a practice which is now greatly discouraged) and the outstretched stance of the legs.

Irish Horses

Irish horses are widely sought after and respected throughout the world; indeed, Ireland is considered to be one of the greatest of all horse-producing countries. Disregarding the Connemara, which is Ireland's native pony (see page 55), the horses for which they are most renowned are the Irish Draught Horse and the Irish Hunter.

The Irish Draught Horse is an old breed, itself probably the result of mixed Spanish, Connemara, and possibly Thoroughbred and heavy horse blood. Crossed now with a Thoroughbred, it produces the Irish Hunter, which commands continual popularity and high prices as a hunter, show jumper and, more recently, an event horse. Many of the horses that have dominated the world of international show jumping in the last couple of decades have been Irish Hunters. They are handsome, bold, good-looking animals, usually standing well over 15.2 h.h. Conformation will vary slightly depending on the parentage, but in general they have fine-looking heads, usually slightly coarser in appearance than a Thoroughbred, good, muscular shoulders, short, strong backs with plenty of heart room, powerful, well-rounded quarters and clean, hard legs. They are noted for their amiable, friendly temperament, good straight action, willingness and endurance.

Whilst the Irish Draught Horse was undoubtedly much used as a harness and work horse at one time, its main purpose in recent years has been as breeding stock for producing Irish half-bloods or hunters. Its energetic, yet free and easy action and its natural talent for jumping seem to be remarkably potent and are continually perpetuated in their offspring. Unfortunately, recent years have seen an increasing shortage of these useful animals—a decline which is keenly felt by breeders and buyers of good horses. Restrictive bans have been imposed on much of the export practices and also on the slaughter of the horses, which was rife at one time, in an attempt to increase the numbers.

British Heavy Horses

In previous centuries, the British heavy horses were bred for two main purposes —as medieval war horses, able to carry knights in heavy armour and as sturdy agricultural workers. Modern methods of warfare and general mechanization obviously greatly affected horses bred for such occupations and at one stage the future of heavy horses looked very bleak. Happily, a strong revival in interest in the heavy horse has helped to reverse this situation. Nowadays their main use is as show animals, favoured particularly by the breweries who use them to pull the old drays on

Left: This prize-winning Suffolk Punch demonstrates to perfection the incredibly compact body with its powerful shoulders and quarters and deep girth that are characteristics of the breed. Note too the crested neck and kindly looking face.

various occasions.

There are three main breeds of heavy horse in Great Britain, the Clydesdale, Shire and Suffolk Punch. Of these, the Shire is the biggest, standing up to an average of 17 h.h., although it is by no means unusual to find them at 18 h.h. Their most notable feature is the abundance of silky hair or 'feather' on the lower part of their legs, and they are generally bay or brown with white markings. Locked into their massive, powerful bodies is immense gentleness and docility. The Shire horse originates from the midland Shire counties and is said to be directly descended from the medieval warhorse or Great Horse, crossed with imported draught horses.

The Clydesdale comes from the Clyde Valley in Lanarkshire, Scotland. It stands about 17 h.h. and may be bay, brown, black and occasionally chestnut, with large areas of white on the body and legs. Again, it carries a lot of feather on the lower part of its legs and is particularly noted for its active, free and straight paces. It also owes much to the medieval Great Horse, but emerged as the recognizable breed of today when farmers began to cross their local haulage mares with heavier Flemish stallions.

As may be supposed, the Suffolk Punch is a native of East Anglia, and of Suffolk in particular. It generally stands about 16 h.h. and is always chestnut, although it can be any one of seven shades of this colour. It is characterized by its dense, immensely compact body with its muscular neck, and massive shoulders and quarters. The clean hard legs carry no feather. Like the Clydesdale and Shire it is kind, honest, and active, but extremely docile and it is renowned for its longevity and outstanding stamina.

The Suffolk Punch dates back to the early sixteenth century when it seems to have emerged naturally as a breed from crosses between the Great Horse and local Norfolk Trotters and cobs. During the eighteenth and nineteenth centuries much care was given to systematic and selective breeding with the result that it is now considered to be one of the purest of all breeds of heavy horse.

Above: Brightly adorned Clydesdales, glittering with traditional horse brasses, take part in a ploughing match.

Below: Besides being seen in the show ring, these Shire horses are also used to make beer deliveries in the vicinity of the brewery.

Horses of the USA

The Mustang

This is the feral descendant of the horses taken to America by the Spanish conquistadores in the early sixteenth century and as such is the oldest of all American breeds. The Spaniards took Andalusian horses with them on their conquest and many of these escaped on to the harsh pampas lands. Natural selection and a need to adapt to the inhospitable surroundings turned them into a tough, wiry little horse, quite different from the fine, proud Andalusian.

Mustangs stand between 14 and 15 h.h.—markedly smaller than their ancestors—and they may be of any colour, although broken colours are perhaps the most common. Lightweight in build and generally undistinguished in appearance, they are the famed mount of the Wild West cowboys and Indians and are still used as cow ponies for everyday work on the ranch. They are also the 'bucking broncos' of the rodeo circuit. Their numbers have dramatically decreased in recent decades, owing mainly to indiscriminate slaughter, but a law passed in 1971 now protects those that still range the pampas lands.

The Quarter Horse

The Quarter Horse is among the most popular breed of horse in the world, with something approaching one million horses registered with the American Quarter Horse Association. This is all the more amazing when it is considered that they were only recognized as a breed at the beginning of 1940. However, they had evolved as a breed long before this, and in fact owe their origin to crosses of the early Spanish horses with those imported from England at the beginning of the seventeenth century.

The Quarter Horse's ability as a working cowhorse is unrivalled, but it owes its name and probably much of its selective breeding to the popular sport of 'match racing'. This was a great favourite with the early farmers and plantation owners and involved racing their horses against one another, usually down the main street of the town. As these streets were rarely more than a quarter-of-a-mile long, the name Quarter Horse was adopted. Even today, there are few other breeds that could touch them over this short distance.

Nowadays, the Quarter Horse is still greatly used on the ranch and for cutting and steer roping contests at rodeos. It has also become internationally sought after as a polo pony, for which its agility and ability to 'turn on a dime' make it ideally suited. Standing about 15.2 h.h., it has a short, broad head set on a fairly short neck and its compact body features a deep chest, strong shoulders, short muscular back and very powerful hindquarters. Its legs are comparatively short, but clean, hard and fine. Quarter Horses may be any solid colour.

The Morgan

The first volume of the Morgan Horse Register was issued in 1850, but the line began with a stallion foaled in Massachusetts somewhere around 1690. Actually named Figure, this stallion ultimately became known as Justin Morgan, which was the name of his schoolmaster owner. Nothing is known for certain of this horse's breeding and he spent his early years doing heavy farm and haulage work. At the same time, he won many weight-pulling contests as well as harness and saddle races held at local, informal gatherings. It

Opposite: Described at one time as 'the glory of the Western Ranges', the Mustang still roams a few areas of the USA wild and free.

Opposite, inset: The bright, perky carriage of the Morgan is well illustrated here. Popular as a riding as well as a harness horse, this is one of the most versatile of all American breeds.

Below: The Quarter Horse is the USA's most popular mount among the ranch cowboys. Besides its amazing agility, so well illustrated here, it is said to possess a natural instinct for working among cattle.

was actually his next owner, recognizing the horse's many talents—and thus his value—who thought of leasing him out to cover local mares. He proved himself to have another invaluable attribute, that of remarkable prepotency, so that in his offspring were reproduced all his essential characteristics of conformation, energetic action, terrific endurance, stamina, strength and great kindness.

The Morgan stands between 14.2 and 15.2 h.h. and is usually brown, black, bay or chestnut. It has a short broad head with small ears and an intelligent face. Its neck is short and very muscular, its shoulders and hindquarters are strong and powerful and its body compact, yet immensely strong. Its alertness and great energy is well displayed in its bright carriage and high, springy action, particularly at the trot. More than any other 'modern' horse breed, the Morgan has influenced horses that have been developed in the USA—in particular the Standardbred, and also the Saddlebred and the Tennessee Walking Horse.

The Saddlebred

Bred by the early settlers in Kentucky, apparently by crossing Thoroughbreds, Morgans, Standardbreds and an obscure breed known as the Narrangensett Pacer, the American Saddlebred was originally used as a general purpose animal for saddle and harness. Nowadays it is bred mainly for the show ring and for this purpose is often trained in two extra gaits—the rack and the slow gait. These are true four-beat gaits in which the hind foot strikes the ground slightly before the forefoot on the same side. The rack in particular, being the faster of the two, is an extremely showy pace to watch, but as it is uncomfortable for a rider and very tiring for a horse over long periods, it is essentially a 'show' pace.

Standing between 15.1 h.h. and 16.1 h.h., the Saddlebred is extremely elegant and distinguished in appearance. Its small refined head is carried high on a proudly-arched, long neck. It has an unusually straight, comparatively long back and long, fine, clean legs. It has a luxuriant, silky mane and tail, the latter often carried unnaturally high, which at one time was the result of cutting the muscles in the dock and resetting the tail in this position. Saddlebreds may be any solid colour and often carry quite extensive white markings on the face or legs.

The Tennessee Walking Horse

Officially recognized as a breed in 1935, the Tennessee Walking Horse, like other American breeds, can trace its beginnings back to the early settlers or Southern plantation owners. All those recognized as Tennessee Walking Horses today can apparently claim direct descent from one stallion, who had both Morgan and Standardbred blood. Foaled in the 1880s, this horse's name was Black Allen.

The distinctive feature of the Tennessee Walking Horse is its unique running walk. This is a superbly comfortable gait in four-time, in which the forefeet touch the ground fractionally before the diagonal hind feet. The forefeet are lifted high off the ground and the hind feet move with a very long stride to produce a rhythmic gliding effect. Undoubtedly originally developed because of the long hours spent in the saddle which demand comfort as a criterion, this pace is now apparently so in-bred into the Tennessee Walking Horse, that

foals seem to perform it almost naturally. It has never been successfully taught to any other breed.

The Tennessee Walking Horse is very good looking. It stands between 15 and 16 h.h. and has a rather long head, with a straight or slightly convex profile. The head is carried high on a long, strong neck, while the long, sloping shoulders and well-muscled quarters account for much of the horse's smooth action. The body is broad and powerful, the back short and the legs clean, hard and fine. Tennessee Walking Horses may be any solid colour.

The Standardbred

This is the principal trotting and pacing racehorse breed of the USA, although it is occasionally also used as a saddle horse. It owes its origin to an admixture of blood, but the founding stallion was a Thoroughbred foaled in Great Britain and imported to Philadelphia towards the end of the eighteenth century. He was crossed with the outstanding harness racing horses of the time (this being judged by their consistent success in races), and produced a succession of foals that were able to trot at racing speeds. The most famous of his descendants was a horse called Hamble-

Opposite and below: The American Saddlebred is another breed characterized by its erect carriage and outstretched stance. It has an unusually high tail carriage which is often accentuated by nicking the dock muscles.

Opposite, inset: This fine Tennessee Walking Horse has been prepared for the show ring. Note how the head is rather plainer and heavier than most of the other American breeds illustrated here.

tonian who did even more than his sire to perpetuate the breed—so much in fact, that his name has become synonymous with the Standardbred. The name of the breed was derived from the decreed speed or 'standard' time laid down in which a horse must cover a measured distance of 1.6 kilometres (1 mile) if he was to qualify for registration in the official American Trotting Register.

The Standardbred's Thoroughbred blood is generally apparent in its appearance, although its heavier bone structure, its longer body and sloping quarters make it better adapted to harness racing than saddle racing. It is therefore slightly less refined in appearance than the Thoroughbred and has a somewhat angular shape. Its average height is 15.2 h.h. and it may be any colour.

Horses of South America

The Criollo

The Criollo is South America's equivalent of the Mustang in that it is descended from the Spanish Andalusians taken into South America by Pedro de Mendoza in 1536. During the sacking of Buenos Aires some time later, many Andalusians escaped into the outlying pampas land, where harsh conditions and natural selection produced a breed of amazingly tough, hardy animals that again bore little resemblance in appearance to their noble ancestors. The Criollo is found in slight variations throughout Uruguay, Brazil, Peru, Chile and Venezuela. In Argentina, where it is known as the Criollo, it is the mount of the gauchos who use it as a pack and cattle horse.

The tough conditions in which this little horse has lived for the last 400 years have given it exceptional resistance to disease, outstanding endurance and stamina and an ability to survive extremes of temperature and a frugal diet. About a century ago, it was extensively crossed with stallions imported from Europe and the USA, which nearly led to the total demise of the breed by undermining its hardiness and toughness. Happily, some breeders realized this before it was too late and a programme of strict, selective breeding was put into practice to re-establish the breed.

The Criollo could equally well be included in the pony breeds that begin on page 52, as it often stands under 14.2 h.h. It is compact, but thickly set, with a large head, muscular neck and a short, straight back. A sandy dun colour, which is said to merge into its arid surroundings, is the most common.

Paso Horses

Representatives of Paso-type horses are found throughout South America and each country naturally claims to have the finest specimens! Like the Criollo, all are descended from the Andalusian horses brought to the continent by the Spanish conquistadores, but the con-

Left: The Peruvian Paso, with its unique lateral four-beat gait, is becoming increasingly popular throughout the USA. It is a small horse with an Arab-type head, as can be seen here.

trolled, selective breeding of these horses has produced a very different result from the Criollo. Paso horses have the proud carriage and noble bearing of their Spanish ancestors. The main characteristic they all have in common is a gait unique to the various Paso breeds. Called the *paso*, it is a pace in four-time in which the legs on one side move together, although the hind-foot strikes the ground a fraction of a second before the forefoot. The forelegs are lifted high off the ground in an extravagant, but smooth action, while the hindlegs take long straight strides. It is known as a lateral—as opposed to diagonal—pace (because of the action of the legs), and it is both extremely comfortable for the rider and remarkably untiring for the horse. The pace may be maintained steadily over great distances. There are three speeds of paso and although the horses can obviously move at the usual paces too, they are generally encouraged by their riders to use one or other of the paso gaits. So

inbred has this movement become in the breed, that the paces appear to be performed naturally and the horses are renowned for being easy to break and train.

Among the most famous of the Paso breeds is the Peruvian Paso, which grows to a maximum of 15 h.h., although it is usually a little smaller than this. It has been bred in Peru for more than 300 years and the rigours of the terrain to be crossed—mountains, deserts and jungles—have produced yet another breed full of stamina and endurance. Thus it shares those inherent characteristics found in the Criollo too, and although it is a strong, sturdy-looking animal, it is considerably more elegant and refined in appearance than its pampas-bred relative.

Pasos from Puerto Rico, Peru and Columbia are known collectively as Paso Finos and under the auspices of the American Paso Fino Horses Association are being inter-bred to produce the ideal Paso type.

Above: Noted above all for its toughness and stamina, the Criollo is South America's native breed. Nowadays, breeders in Argentina subject stallions to a rigorous endurance test before selecting them finally for breeding.

Horses of Scandinavia

The Swedish Half-Bred sometimes called the Swedish Warm Blood

This horse, first bred as a cavalry horse, is now one of the most successful competition horses in international events in the fields of dressage, show jumping and eventing. Originally descended from native mares crossed with imported stallions, many of which had Oriental blood, much was done by the Swedish government to improve the breed at the beginning of the century. It financed two studs and imported Thoroughbred and German stallions, the aim being to produce horses of good conformation and intelligence, combined with a keenly developed athletic ability. Rigorous standards and examinations are imposed and strict controls exercised over the breeding, which has resulted in an extremely good-looking

saddle horse that stands about 16.2 h.h. It has a neat, refined head, a well-proportioned neck and body and combines great strength with great gentleness and docility.

The North Swedish Horse

A decendant of small native mares, no attempt was made to standardize this light draught-type horse until the end of the nineteenth century when a breed society was formed. Breeding became strictly controlled, mainly using Norwegian Døle stallions (see page 37), and within a decade or so, a type was established.

Greatly favoured for work in forestry and agriculture, as well as a one-time artillery horse used by the army, the North Swedish Horse stands about 15.2 h.h. and is a muscular, strong-

Opposite, centre: Note the thick mane and tail which are characteristics of the North Swedish Horse.

Opposite, bottom: A Swedish Warmblood photographed at the government-financed state stud in Flyinge, Sweden.

Below: This Finnish horse has the characteristic kindly, honest face.

A Finnish mare and foal. The chestnut colour seen opposite is more common than a dun coat colour.

framed horse of medium build with exceptionally strong legs. It is lively, willing and energetic, noted for its good temperament and inherent soundness. Its lively gait, particularly at the trot, has gained it some reputation as a trotter and trotting races with these horses are popular in the northern part of Sweden. Although careful selective breeding has taken place, using the most consistently successful proven trotters, to produce a slightly lighter type of horse (known as the North Swedish Trotter), it is not in the same league as trotters from the USA, USSR, or those bred elsewhere in Europe.

The Swedish Ardennes

This is Sweden's heavy draught horse, which in common with many other draught horses around the world is declining in numbers as mechanization renders it more and more redundant. It is very similar to the Belgian Ardennes horse (see page 40), from which it is descended. Belgian Ardennes were imported into Sweden in the nineteenth century and crossed with the North Swedish Horse to produce this strong, active, muscular but compactly built, animal. Standing between 15.2 and 16 h.h. and renowned for its longevity, kindness and hardness, its principal use now is in hauling timber in remote forest areas.

The Fredericksborg

This is Denmark's oldest indigenous breed and was developed in the mid-sixteenth century. It takes its name from King Frederick II who founded the Fredericksborg Stud to provide horses for the European royal stables. The breed was produced using Spanish (in the form of Andalusian) and Italian stock and, later, Arab and Thoroughbred blood was added, too. Before long the Fredericksborg was considered to be the most elegant riding horse in Europe and was so popular that the stud was unable to meet the demand. This led to its being disbanded in the early nineteenth century and it was not until the beginning of this century that the breed began to be registered again. It is unlikely that the modern Fredericksborg bears much resemblance to its forbears, as the few that remained to perpetuate the breed have been widely crossed with horses of other breeds and blood. Nowadays it stands about 15.3 h.h. and is a well-built animal with notably powerful shoulders, big chest, very deep girth, broad back and muscular quarters. Nearly always some shade of chestnut, it is used today for light draught and harness work and also as a riding horse.

The Knabstrup

The spotted Knabstrup, also from Denmark, is said to date back to the Napoleonic wars. At this time, a chestnut mare which had spotted 'blanket' markings (see page 21) and proved itself to have outstanding qualities of speed and endurance was put to a Fredericksborg palomino-coloured stallion. The resulting foal, which was spotted like its dam, became the founding stallion of the Knabstrup breed. Today the Knabstrup greatly resembles the Fredericksborg in appearance and conformation, although it is generally slightly lighter in build. Always spotted in the same patterns as the Appaloosa (see page 21), it has always been popular as a circus horse.

The Jutland

Denmark's other main breed of horse is the Jutland—a heavy cart-horse type, whose history goes back at least eight centuries. Used extensively over that time for agriculture and haulage work, it was also the Danish war horse of the Middle Ages. Those in existence today are said to have been strongly influenced by the Suffolk Punch, which was imported into Denmark in the mid-nineteenth century. The Jutland is usually chestnut, and has the docile temperament and typical build of a heavy draught horse. It stands between 15.2 and 16 h.h., making it slightly smaller than the British heavy horses.

The Døle

The Norwegian Døle is the most widespread horse in Norway and, owing to regular infusions of outside blood from a number of breeds, it varies greatly in conformation and type. In general it is similar in build and appearance to the Dales Pony of Britain (although a little taller, standing on average about 15 h.h.), and the two are believed to have descended from common Northern stock. Characteristics of the breed are a squarish, neat, pony-type head, well-crested neck, strong, long back with short legs and powerful shoulders and quarters. Varying as it does in type, it can, and does, fulfil a number of different purposes, from haulage, agricultural and forestry work to pleasure riding and trotting. Its good straight action, particularly at the trot, has led to the development of an 'offshoot' breed known as the Døle Trotter. A Thoroughbred stallion, imported in 1834, apparently exercised great influence on the lighter types of Døle, which quickly became much in demand as attractive harness horses for light vehicles. The popularity of trotting races grew, so that the Trotter became sufficiently numerous to be recognized as a breed. Trotters of other breeds were also introduced to improve the qualities necessary in a competitive trotting horse.

Opposite, top: The Norwegian Døle varies in build from a fairly light-weight pony to a strong draught type.

Opposite, bottom: The Fredericks-borg has powerful shoulders, deep girth and rounded barrel.

Below: Throughout its history, the Knabstrup has been crossed with a variety of breeds, so that it now varies greatly in type.

Horses of France

The Selle Française

A number of types of horse is now included in this overall title, which generally refers to the highly successful French competition horse. It is the result of various crosses between native work mares and Thoroughbreds, Arabs, Barbs and trotters, as well as stallions from Germany and Scandinavia. Included under the umbrella title is, for example, the Anglo-Norman, a horse developed in the early nineteenth century in Normandy, originally as a light harness horse and trotter. It found favour with the cavalry as well as being a general saddle horse. Standing about 16 h.h., it is a good-looking, compact horse of excellent conformation with great jumping ability. It is known, too, as the French Saddle Horse.

Other departments in France all breed equivalents of the Anglo-Norman, which have slight variations but are all basically similar in type. The breeding of horses in France is carefully controlled by the French government, who own nearly all the stallions in the country, whatever their type.

The French Trotter

This breed of horse also originated from Normandy and is an offshoot of the Anglo-Norman (which contained Norfolk Trotter blood) when crossed with English Thoroughbreds and American stallions. Trotting races are extremely popular in France. The first one ever was held in Cherbourg in 1836 and the French Trotter was developed at this time. Selective breeding continued, with infusions of such blood as the famous Russian trotting horse, the Orlov. In 1941, a ruling decreed that only foals of horses previously registered in the stud book would be officially recognized. Since then, the breed has remained remarkably pure.

The French Trotter is of light build, but standing at about 16.2 h.h., is taller than most other trotting breeds. This is because trotting races in France are sometimes ridden, rather than run in harness, which means the horses must also be able to carry weights over a distance at speed. France is the only country that runs trotting races under saddle.

Below: A magnificent example of the heavy draught-type Breton. Note its short, crested neck, deep, strong body and short but clean legs.

French Heavy Horses

France has a number of heavy draught horses, among them the Auxois, the Comtois, the Poitevin, the Ardennes, the Percheron, the Boulonnais and the Breton. The last four are the best known and most widespread.

The Ardennes, of which there are two types, is also found extensively in Belgium (see page 40). In France, it is bred in the north-east and is an immensely strong, but compactly built horse with short, exceptionally thick, legs. The type found near Chaumont is noticeably smaller than the more widely distributed Belgian type and stands only about 15 h.h.

The Percheron is perhaps the best known of all the French heavy horses and is now bred in many other countries too. It originated in the Perche district of France, where native mares from the Parisian Basin were crossed with various stallions, noticeably those possessing Oriental and Norman blood. The breed of today also has a lot of pure Arab blood in its veins which probably accounts for its unusually elegant appearance and such points as its small refined head and silky coat. Standing up to 17 h.h., Percherons are certainly impressive to look at. Their normal coat colours of either grey or black enhance their imposing appearance.

The Boulonnais is similar to the Percheron in appearance and also has much Oriental blood in its ancestry. Apart from the Arab, this is said to have come from Roman cavalry horses taken to France in the first century, from horses taken to the country during the Crusades and by an Andalusian strain introduced in the Middle Ages. Noted for its lively energetic paces, it is usually grey and can stand up to 17 h.h. It is found mainly in north-western France.

The Breton comes from Brittany and there are at least two types. The heavier sort owes its great bulk and weight to infusions of Percheron, Boulonnais and Ardennes blood, while the lighter type was developed through crosses with Norfolk Trotters during the nineteenth century. Both stand between 15 and 16 h.h. and are bred as coach and draught horses, as well as for agricultural purposes.

Above: A French Trotter foal demonstrates already its light pronounced trotting paces. The characteristic long legs of the breed may be seen in both foal and dam.

39

Horses of Belgium and Holland

The Ardennes

As we have already seen, this horse is also a French breed. The larger of the two types is found principally in Belgium and owes its greater weight and height to infusions of Brabant blood (see below). It is an old breed, said to have been known and valued during Caesar's time and has found constant favour over the centuries as a cavalry and artillery horse. It is one of the most hardy of all heavy draught horses, a characteristic well illustrated during the Napoleonic wars, when it was able to endure the extremely harsh conditions that were to prove too much for many other breeds. In addition, it is energetic, yet extremely docile. Principal colours are bay, roan or chestnut.

The Brabant

Known also as the Belgian Heavy Draught Horse, this is Belgium's other indigenous breed of horse. It comes from the low-lying areas of Belgium, where the conditions for breeding and keeping horses are excellent. As a result, it is an imposing horse that is massive, yet compact, in appearance. The Brabant of today, which invariably breeds true to type, developed towards the end of the nineteenth century, when the Cheval du Trait Belge Association was formed to protect the purity and uniformity of the breed. The breed as such, however, existed long before this time, and is variously acclaimed as being the medieval Great Horse, as having been used by Caesar and as being descended from a 'large horse' that existed some two million years ago! It has had a marked influence on many of the world's cold-blooded breeds.

The Gelderland

This horse gets its name from the Dutch province of Gelderland, although it is now popular throughout Holland. It originated by crossing native mares with a variety of stallions, notably Thoroughbreds and French and German horses. Attempts have been centred in recent decades on producing a standard type of Gelderland, with the result that it has now become a good saddle and show horse, a show jumper to be reckoned with, and an excellent pleasure harness animal. It stands about 16 h.h. and is usually chestnut or

grey. It has a good, if plain head, a well-muscled, arched neck and a broad, deep body. Its shoulders are long and sloping, its hindquarters powerful and its legs strong and clean.

The Friesian

Emanating from the Province of Friesland in Holland, the Friesian is an extremely handsome, black animal (the only other marking permitted is a small white star on its face). An old breed, it was used in the Middle Ages as a war horse and later found favour both as a charger and a saddle horse. The Friesian has undoubtedly had infusions of Andalusian and Oriental blood, which would help to account for its pleasing appearance.

In the early part of this century, the

Above: The powerful Dutch Draught Horse is noted for its seemingly endless stamina. In spite of its heavy build, it is extremely active and renowned as a hard worker.

Left: The Brabant, which stands up to 17 hands high, is most frequently coloured red roan with black mane, tail and legs as the one illustrated here.

popularity of the breed greatly declined, to such an extent, in fact, that in 1913 there were only three registered stallions. However, a society was formed to preserve the breed and it underwent a great revival in World War II when the short supply of motorized transport, coupled with fuel rationing, meant alternative forms of transport had to be sought. Friesians were then much in demand because of their great versatility as agricultural workers as well as being good harness and saddle horses. Standing up to about 15 h.h., the Friesian has a strong but compact body and good energetic paces.

The Dutch Draught Horse

This is one of the most massive of all European heavy horses and the breed was created by crossing native mares with Belgian heavy draught stallions. For the last five decades or so, only horses of known pedigree have been registered in the stud book. In consequence it is the only breed in Holland in which the breeding has been kept absolutely pure. The Dutch Draught Horse stands up to about 16.2 h.h., and is usually of a chestnut, bay or grey colour. Like most heavy horses, it is particularly noted for its equable, willing and docile nature.

Above left: The Ardennes stallion provides an excellent example of the extremely compact yet muscular body and short legs of the breed. It also has a thicker, shorter neck than most other breeds of heavy horse.

Above: This leggy Friesian colt has not yet developed the sturdier build characteristics of the breed. As it matures, its body will become considerably deeper and stronger to give a more overall compact appearance.

Left: The Dutch Gelderland is popular as a riding mount as well as a carriage horse. The slightly convex face of the breed may be seen in the mare pictured here.

Horses of Germany

The Holstein

Among the oldest of all German breeds, Holsteins were known to be popular as war horses in the Middle Ages. The apparent result of native mares being crossed with imported stallions (notably Spanish Andalusians brought in after the Reformation), the Holstein has more recently received infusions of Thoroughbred blood together with that of other quality riding horses. Thus its centuries-old role as a carriage horse has changed, and it is now widely popular as a riding horse, showing particular aptitude for jumping and eventing.

It stands at least up to 16.2 h.h. and generally varies from light to dark brown. It is described as being a 'large-framed, vigorous, deep, broad horse' and has a long, straight head often featuring a Roman nose. Over the centuries, the Holstein has been instrumental in the founding and developing

Below: Although now extremely popular as a saddle horse, particularly for show jumping and eventing, the tall Oldenburg is also greatly sought after as a carriage horse.

of many important European breeds, of which the Hanoverian (below) is one.

The Hanoverian

This strong saddle horse was developing during the seventeenth and eighteenth centuries. It received a considerable fillip from the British Hanoverian kings, beginning during the reign of George I when the Central Stud was founded at Celle. Hanoverians were used from that time until the reign of George V to pull the English royal coaches. Like the Holstein, it has received recent infusions from Thoroughbred blood in order to produce a breed that meets the contemporary demand for a riding, rather than a harness, horse. The Hanoverian of today has proved itself an immense success in this regard, and will be seen competing in all branches of international equestrianism, show jumping in particular. It stands between 16 and 17 h.h. and may be any solid colour. It has excellent conformation, featuring a somewhat plain head, long neck, powerful shoulders and hindquarters and a muscular, compact body. It possesses great intelligence and courage which makes it an ideal competition horse.

The German nation have placed great emphasis on breeding both power and an equable temperament into their riding horses, and control is exercised over horse breeding by regional associations. One result of this is that differences between the saddle breeds are becoming less apparent so that an overall German Riding Horse type is beginning to emerge.

The Mecklenburg

The Mecklenburg is closely related to the Hanoverians, a breed which it was responsible in part for founding. At one time they were one of Germany's principal breeds and were favoured by Napoleon's army as remounts. Unlike other German breeds so far discussed, it suffered rather than benefitted from infusions of Thoroughbred blood, which was introduced indiscriminately.

The Oldenburg

This is probably the heaviest of all the German riding horses, but the lighter specimens have proved very successful in eventing and show jumping. The Friesian was the main progenitor of the breed, which was founded during the seventeenth century. Great influence

was exercised upon it by Spanish, Italian and English stallions in the late eighteenth century. Throughout the 1880s the Oldenburg was popular as a fashionable carriage horse, as well as a good, general-purpose utility animal. When mechanization lessened the demand for it in such respects, more 'foreign blood' was introduced into the breed from the Thoroughbred and Cleveland Bays, as well as from French and other German breeds. The aim–successfully achieved–was to produce a quality riding horse.

Nowadays the Oldenburg stands about 17 h.h. and is most commonly bay, black or brown. Its conformation is excellent.

Top: The Holstein. This good all-purpose horse is equally at home under saddle as in harness.

Above: The Hanoverian is among the oldest of all German warm breeds. It is responsible for helping to upgrade many other breeds, and is popular as a harness and saddle horse.

The Trakhener

The Trakhener breed actually originated from East Prussia and it is sometimes known as the East Prussian. The famous Trakhener Stud, where the breed was largely developed, was founded in 1732 by William I of Prussia, in what was then the north-western part of the province. The breed was developed using a small native horse, but it was considerably improved at the beginning of the nineteenth century by crossing it with Arab and Thoroughbred stallions.

Up to World War II, East Prussia was the biggest horse breeding centre of the German Reich. A famous story tells of how a number of stallions and in-foal mares were taken from the stud during the winter of 1945 when word came that the Russians were advancing. The 1500 kilometre (900 mile) journey into West

Germany was undertaken through appalling winter weather conditions, and the fact that the horses actually survived gives an indication of their amazing stamina and endurance. The 'refugees' were used to perpetuate the

Left: Another good all-purpose German horse, the Trakhener, is bred extensively on private studs in West Germany. It is attractive and active, as the illustration shows.

Below: A stud farm in Marbach, Germany where riders may go for instructional courses. These riders are mounted on quality German-bred saddle horses.

breed in Germany, and it is now considered by many people to be the best of the current West German breeds. An extremely good-looking, elegant animal, noted for its inherent soundness and strong constitution, the Trakhener stands between 16 and 16.2 h.h. It has excelled in show jumping and dressage, as well as finding success as a show hack.

The German Trotter

The German Trotter was founded as a breed using the famous Russian Orlov Trotter, the first stud being established in Germany in 1885. Although trotting races are more popular in Germany than saddle racing, breeding of these horses is carried out privately, with owners possessing just one or two mares. The breed has been greatly upgraded by the introduction of 'trotting' blood from American Standardbreds and French Trotters. It stands about 15.3 h.h. and has a bold but tractable nature. Its long body has muscular hindquarters and well-developed shoulders and has superb movement and a long-striding action. Horses must reach speeds of 1 minute 30 seconds over a distance of 1000 metres (1100 yards) before they are eligible for registration in the recognized racing entry book.

German Heavy Horses

The two most common types of heavy horses found in Germany are the Schleswig and the Rhineland or Rhenish Heavy Draught. The Schleswig is found in the northern part of West Germany and is closely related to Denmark's Jutland horse, a breed which it closely resembles. However, it has had infusions of blood from other breeds – among them Suffolk Punches, Breton, Boulonnais and even Thoroughbred – as well as consistent interbreeding with Danish stallions. A stud book was opened to exercise more rigorous control in 1891 and is still in existence today. Standing about 15.3 h.h., the stocky, dense Schleswig is noted for being kind and willing. Its easy, smooth movement made it popular during the nineteenth century for pulling buses and streetcars.

The Rhineland Heavy Draught is another good-natured heavy horse which was developed at the end of the nineteenth century to meet the demands for horses wanted in agriculture and

industry. At one time, there were more of this breed in Germany than any other type of horse, although it was known by various regional names. It is very similar to the Belgian Brabant in appearance, although it usually stands a little smaller. Traditionally it has a light reddish brown coloured coat, with a slightly lighter coloured mane and tail.

Above top: A typically coloured Schleswig Heavy Draught.

Above: A German Trotter. The fine hard legs account for its long-striding action.

Horses of Austria, Spain and Portugal

The Lippizanas

This is the famous 'high school' horse of the Spanish Riding School in Vienna. It takes its name from Lippiza, near Trieste, which is where Archduke Charles founded the original stud in 1510 with the purpose of providing horses for court use. The breed was developed by crossing the local light war-type horse with Spanish stallions, and later some Arab blood was introduced into the breed. It is said that five out of the six famous 'strains' of Lippizana perpetuated today in Austria originated in the sixteenth or early seventeenth century. Progeny from the individual strains are identified by the various names which are used as prefixes to their names.

The Spanish Riding School at Vienna was founded in 1735 by Charles VI and it is here that stallions of the Lippizana breed are still taught the magnificent high school movements, known as 'airs above the ground'. All Austrian Lippizanas are bred nowadays at the stud in Piber and stallions that excel in the high school disciplines will return there for stud.

Lippizanas are almost invariably grey, the foals being born black. The coat lightens in colour as they mature. They are majestic in appearance, standing about 16 h.h. The superb conformation, springy trot with high knee action and an innate intelligence and willingness to learn, are the factors that make them so suited to high school work. Lippizanas are also bred at a number of studs in Hungary and Yugoslavia where, as in Austria, breeding is strictly controlled by the governments.

The Andalusian

This is a very old breed of horse which has exerted more influence over the warm-blooded breeds of the world than almost any other type, except the Arab. Its own origin is uncertain, although Spaniards claim there have been horses in the Iberian Peninsula since long before the Roman invasion. Thus the

Below: An Alter Real dressed in the traditional, richly embroidered saddle cloth and quilted saddle ready for the bull ring. The ornate bridle has plumes attached to the head-piece and colourful ribbons adorn the horse's tail.

Below, inset: Austrain Lippizanas indulge in playful antics when given their freedom in these lush pastures.

Left: The beautiful Andalusian from Spain is nearly always grey, although not necessarily dappled. Well illustrated here are the characteristic convex face, strong crested neck, powerful, compact body and clean, strong legs.

Andalusian is said to be wholly Spanish, with no 'foreign' blood at all. However, at various periods throughout its history, horses from Africa and others of eastern origin – probably Barbs (see page 49) – have been brought to Spain and would undoubtedly have bred with the local horses, although it must be admitted that the breeding of Andalusians has always been carried out with the utmost care and selectivity. Among the greatest and most fanatical breeders of all were the Carthusian monks, who jealously guarded their beautiful horses at Jerez, at a time when the breed was experiencing a number of problems elsewhere in the country. Today Andalusians stand about 16 h.h. and are nearly always grey. They are described as being a medium-sized, elegant, fairly light saddle horse, that is intelligent, proud and possesses a fiery temperament. Pure-bred Andalusians are something of a rarity now, even in Spain, and they are greatly prized. They may be seen in carnivals and parades, giving displays of *haute école* and, occasionally, as the mounts of top bullfighters. They are also highly favoured as circus horses.

The Alter Real

This elegant saddle horse, also much used in *haute école*, is one of the Andalusian's finest descendants. It was developed as a breed in the mid-eighteenth century, when some 300 of the finest Andalusians were used to found a National Stud. The stud flourished for a hundred years during which time it supplied horses to the royal manège in Lisbon, where they were trained in similar disciplines to those of the Spanish Riding School at Vienna. Indiscriminate breeding with Arabs, Thoroughbreds and other foreign blood at a time when the country was in the midst of political upheaval and turmoil in the latter part of the nineteenth century, almost brought about the demise of the breed. The Ministry of Economy took over the stud in 1932 and began an intensive programme to reinstate the breed. Even today, however, there are few Alter Reals of top quality in Portugal.

At its best, the horse stands about 15.2 h.h. and is generally bay or brown. It has excellent conformation and naturally high, showy action. As might be expected, it is very similar in appearance to the Andalusian.

The Lusitano

This is Portugal's other popular breed, much favoured for mounted bullfighting. It is an old breed, whose origins are rather obscure, although it is believed again to be related to the Andalusian. It stands about 15.2 h.h. and is noted for its intelligence and courage, as well as its agility and speed.

Horses of the Middle East and North Africa

The Arab

Although now established and bred in nearly all the horse owning and breeding countries of the world, this most beautiful of all horses emanated from the deserts of Arabia. One eighth-century historian is said to have traced Arab pedigrees right back to the time of Noah's great-great-great-grandson, while records of named Arab horses, dating back some 5000 years, have been found. Many legends are attached to the Arab, one of which says that all pure-blood Arab horses can trace their ancestry back to the seven mares of the Prophet. Another says that Allah created the horse out of the South Wind. Its origins, although obscure, are, unfortunately, likely to be considerably more prosaic!

Careful, selective breeding of the Arab has taken place over many centuries. The Bedouins were known to be practising it at the time of Mohammed in the seventh century, but there is evidence which points to the fact that it was going on long before this time too. Great attention has always been paid to preserving the purity of line, and this, combined with the rigours and hardships of the Arab's natural habitat, go a long way to ex-

plaining its all-round supremacy among horse breeds today.

No other breed in the world has influenced and founded so many breeds of horse and pony. Undoubtedly, its most important progeny is the English Thoroughbred, but it has in fact influenced, if not directly participated in, the development of practically every breed of warm-blooded horse alive today.

Although conformation of the Arab varies slightly according to its type, to the characteristics preferred and emphasized by its breeders, and to the conditions of its habitat, all Arabs have some basic factors in common. The head is small and exceptionally fine, with a pronounced concave or 'dished' profile and a noticeably small muzzle. The ears are neat and perfectly formed, and the eyes are large, dark and intelligent, capable of displaying great fieriness. The nostrils are large and flaring. The head is carried high on a longish, beautifully-arched neck which slopes into generally rather high withers. The body is always neat and compact and the legs sinewy and finely chiselled. The most common coat colours are grey and chestnut and Arabs usually stand between 14.2 and 15 h.h. Other notable

Opposite, top: This Anglo-Arab hack shows its Arabian heritage in its refined head, and its Thoroughbred heritage in its overall conformation.

Opposite, bottom: The intelligent, kindly face of a Barb. Note the straight profile in comparison to the more concave nose of the Anglo-Arab above.

Below: A beautiful Arabian stallion grazing. Even at rest the tail carriage is high. These exquisite horses are bred throughout the world and many countries have developed their own particular strain of the breed.

characteristics are their exceptionally soft skin, particularly around the muzzle, and fine silky coat. The mane and tail, too, are extremely fine and silky and the tail is carried high, so it streams out like a banner. The Arab's movements and paces are particularly fluid and harmonious, with light springy strides and straight action.

The Anglo-Arab

Compared with the Arab, this breed is still in its infancy, for it was developed by crossing Arabs with Thoroughbreds —the latter not existing itself as a breed until some 250 years ago. Anglo-Arabs have been bred most successfully and systematically in France and also in Poland, although they are bred in other countries, too.

To be recognized as a true Anglo-Arab, there must be at least twenty-five percent Arab blood present, although the best specimens usually have more. The crossing of these two magnificent breeds should, in theory, produce a superb riding horse and indeed, in most instances, this is what does happen. Although the appearance will vary somewhat according to such factors as which parent's characteristics were the most dominant, there is a definite type of horse recognized as the Anglo-Arab. It stands between 15 and 16 h.h. and is most usually bay or chestnut. It is described as being an elegant, light riding horse with a delicate head, usually straight-profiled, a long, arched neck, short, well-shaped body and long slender legs. It has excelled in the competitive fields of dressage, eventing and jumping and is much sought after as a hack and hunter.

The Barb

The Barb, which comes from North Africa, has long been linked with the Arab. The two breeds have been interbred since the eighth century to such an extent that there are few pure-bred Barbs in existence today. The Barb, too, is a horse that has exerted constant influence over other breeds and it has been the foundation stock of many of the world's warm-blooded horses. Many Barbs were imported into Britain during the reign of Charles II, who used them to improve British racehorses. Thus it was also instrumental in founding the English Thoroughbred.

A pure-bred Barb stands between 14 and 15 h.h. and may be any solid colour.

It has a long head with a convex profile, flat shoulders, a short back and steeply sloping quarters. Like the Arab, it has an exceptionally strong constitution and great stamina and powers of endurance.

Horses of Australia and Russia

The Waler

Australia has no indigenous horses and yet the early settlers desperately needed them to provide transport over the huge areas of their new homeland. The first horses were all imported and appear to have comprised a mixture of horses brought from South Africa and a variety of cob, pony and draught types from different countries in Europe. Thoroughbreds, Arabs and probably Barbs were also among the early horses found there too. The result of this great admixture of blood was the Waler—a hardy, tough, strong animal that stood up to 16 h.h. and had a deep well-ribbed body, a sensible head, long legs and a reputation for great powers of endurance. As well as providing an ideal horse to cope with the rigours of the Australian outback, the Waler was a great favourite with the Indian Army and regular shipments left Australia. During World War I they were in demand, too, as artillery horses and cavalry remounts. Unfortunately, the Australian quarantine laws forbade the re-entry of these horses and thousands had to be destroyed as a result.

With its use now mainly confined only to ranch and agricultural work, breeding of the Waler in Australia nevertheless still continues. However, it has evolved into a new breed, different from the Waler of yesteryear, and known now as The Australian Stockhorse. An official register has been opened with the aim of establishing a fixed type.

The Brumby

The Brumby is Australia's 'wild' horse, although of course it can only have descended from domestic stock. During the gold rush of the mid-nineteenth century, when the new excitement and allure of instant riches meant many people neglected their farms, horses were correspondingly less important in the lives of the settlers. Many of them escaped or strayed from the poorly fenced homesteads, while others were turned out loose on the ranges. Of course, only the fittest and most cunning survived and developed into a race of horses that have no equal in toughness and native 'low cunning'. So numerous did these bush horses become, that later, after the gold rush had died down, they began to be a threat to newly-established farmers. They broke through fences, trampled over crops, drank the precious water supplies and enticed domestic stock away to a life of freedom. As a result, 'Brumby runners' sprang up—men who rounded up these wild animals, driving them into temporary stockyards for slaughter, or in a few cases, for training as stock horses or for use in rodeos.

The Orlov

Russia is extremely rich in native horse breeds, many of which are scarcely known outside the country. Probably the most famous of all of them, and the most widely known of all Soviet breeds, is the Orlov, developed in the late eighteenth century by Count Alexei Orlov. He mated an Arab stallion with a Danish-bred mare. The resulting colt foal was later crossed with a Dutch mare to produce a stallion called Bars I. This is considered to be the true founding horse of the Orlov breed. Since then, the breed has been improved by adding Arab, Thoroughbred and Norfolk Trotter blood. In this century, Standardbreds from America have also been introduced in order to produce a really top quality trotting horse.

Orlovs stand about 15.3 h.h. and are powerful and comparatively thick-set. Usually grey or black, they have a luxuriant mane and tail and very hard legs. They possess excellent action and a strong constitution and are noted for their longevity.

Opposite: Horsemen chase a Brumby herd on high mountain slopes in the Snowy Mountains of New South Wales, Australia.

Below: The most famous of all the Russian horses is the Orlov and the one shown here is typical of the breed.

Ponies of the British Isles

The Shetland

This is the smallest of all British native breeds and comes from the group of Islands from which it takes its name, off the northern coast of Scotland. It is a very old breed, the origins of which are lost in antiquity, although it was known to be living in the Shetland Islands by 500 BC. Its superlative strength, which is so great it is in no way commensurate with its size, has meant it has been used for all sorts of work on the farm, in harness, and as a pack animal, for centuries. It was also once much in demand as a pit pony. On average, Shetlands stand about 10 h.h. and may be any colour. They have a small, well-shaped head, a deep thick-set body and strong, short legs. In winter, they seem almost to disappear beneath an immensely thick, woolly coat and a long, thick mane and tail.

The Highland

The Highland pony is Scotland's other native pony breed and there are two recognized types. The mainland type, known also as the Garron, is the taller of the two, standing up to 14.2 h.h. and is the most widely known. The Western Isles type varies in height from 12.2 to 14.2 h.h., and is often regarded as being the purer strain. This type—particularly those that come from the Isle of Rhum— often display the characteristic dun or cream coat colouring which appears to have a silvery outer layer. Silver hairs also abound in the otherwise black mane and tail. In general, both Highland types are powerful, well-built animals with short, broad heads, cresty necks and compact muscular bodies. They are used as all-purpose utility animals by the Highland farmers and crofters and their sure-footedness, willingness to work, docile nature and immense stamina make them ideal for work over rough, often inhospitable terrain. Traditionally associated with deer-stalking, they have found great favour more recently as trekking mounts.

The Dales

The Dales pony is the most northern of all English breeds, and is found to the east of the Pennine range of hills. Large and stocky, it stands up to 14.2 h.h. and has a powerful, muscular body. Such

Above: A round-barrelled Shetland pony mare stands protectively with her fluffy foal. The Shetland is one of the best loved British pony breeds.

Left: The intelligent face of a Highland pony. Dun is the most common colour, but these ponies may also be grey, chestnut, bay or black.

strength combined with stamina and docility makes it invaluable as a work animal on the farm, in the mines and as a pack pony as well as for all sorts of haulage and harness work and riding. Mechanization this century considerably changed the life of the Dales, rendering it redundant to such an extent that the breed fell into marked decline. However, the advent and growing popularity of pony trekking, to which the Dales' temperament and surefootedness makes it ideally suited, has revived a great deal of interest in the breed.

The Fell

The Fell pony is found in an area southwest of the Dales in Cumberland and Westmoreland. In many respects it resembles the Dales pony, although it is a little smaller (it must not exceed 14 h.h.), and, indeed, they are both primarily of Celtic descent. It too, has a history of work on the farm and as a general harness pony. It was also greatly used in the seventeenth and eighteenth centuries to carry lead from the mines to the east coast ports. Its smooth, fast trot made it popular for trotting races organized by local farmers as weekend relaxation. Nowadays it is principally a pleasure riding pony and is often used as foundation stock for crossing with Thoroughbreds to produce quality hunters and jumpers.

The Welsh Mountain

The Welsh Stud Book is divided into four sections, covering the Welsh Mountain Pony, the Welsh Pony, the Welsh Pony of Cob Type, and the Welsh Cob. Of these, the Welsh Mountain Pony is the best known and is also the foundation stock for the others. It is one of the prettiest of all native breeds, and was already breeding wild on the Welsh hills at the time of the Roman occupation. Oriental blood was introduced by the Romans, and in the last three centuries Arabs have also been crossed with the ponies. This no doubt accounts for their appearance: they are often referred to as miniature Arabs. They display such 'arab' features as a small neat head with convex profile and neat, pointed ears, a compact muscular body, high-set tail that is carried gaily, and good free, energetic action. Welsh Mountain Ponies should not exceed 12 h.h. and may be any colour except piebald and skewbald.

Above, top: Dales ponies, often jet black or dark brown, are known locally as heckberry.

Above: Welsh Mountain Pony mares and foals. Grey is a common coat colour.

Left: The Fell pony is usually black and should not display any white markings.

53

The New Forest
New Forest ponies have inhabited the wooded area of that same name in central, southern England for close on 1000 years. Throughout that time, however, ponies of varying types have also been turned out in the forest, so that the blood of these ponies has become very mixed. Besides some Thoroughbred influence, there have been infusions of native breeds, and also Arab and Hackney. Not all of these improved the breed and indeed had the result of breeding out some of the natural inherent toughness and ability to survive harsh, winter weather conditions. The New Forest Pony Breeding and Cattle Society has made strong attempts to exercise some control over the breeding, so that a definite type is becoming fixed. It varies in height from 12 to 14.2 h.h., and has a longish head, a short neck and back with a deep girth and strong hindquarters. New Forest ponies make excellent children's mounts, particularly as they are friendly, willing and docile. In addition, accustomed as they are to the streams of cars that continually drive along the forest roads, they are almost invariably 'traffic-proof'.

The Exmoor
The Exmoor is the oldest breed of all Britain's native ponies, and is known to have been in existence in the south west of the country in prehistoric times. It is sometimes said to have been instrumental in helping to found the Thoroughbred; be that as it may, it is considered by many people to produce the finest hunter types when crossed with the Thoroughbred today.

Exmoors must not exceed 12.3 h.h. and are characterized by their dull, wiry-textured winter coat, which may be bay, brown or dun, and their 'mealy'-coloured muzzle. They are intelligent, hardy and tough—characteristics well displayed by their ability to survive on the inhospitable moor; in winter, the moor is often buried under snow and offers little natural protection from harsh weather.

The Dartmoor
A near relative of the Exmoor, the Dartmoor pony inhabits an area of similar terrain and conditions, a little to the south. In accordance with its environment, it has similar qualities of toughness, stamina and an ability to

Above: The 'mealy-muzzled' Exmoor peers out at the photographer from beneath a thick thatch of forelock. In times of hardship, it will even eat the prickly gorse.

Opposite, top: The pretty Connemara is now widely sought as a child's riding pony and has a natural aptitude for jumping.

Opposite, bottom: Dartmoor mares and foals graze among the rocky outcrops of their moorland home. The characteristic abundant mane is much in evidence here!

survive immense adversity. It is not such an old breed as the Exmoor and has also suffered considerably by infusions of blood from other breeds and types. World War II also had disastrous effects on the Dartmoor, when its native home was used as a training ground for the army.

The formation of a stud book and a breed society has helped to stabilize the breed which must not exceed 12.2 h.h. and is usually bay, black or brown with very few white markings. It has a compact body and small head, with remarkably tiny ears, and its kind, tractable nature makes it an ideal child's first pony.

The Connemara

This is the beautiful native pony of Ireland, found in the western region of the same name. It is an old breed, believed to have descended from primitive native stock, breeding later with Spanish horses said to have swum ashore from the wrecks of the Spanish Armada. Arab and Thoroughbred blood have also been introduced, with the aim of producing a quality riding pony.

The Connemara is a very pretty pony, with a refined, proudly-carried head, neatly arched neck and long, straight back. Its body is compact and muscular. At one time the typical colour was dun, but there are few such coloured specimens in existence now, and the predominant colour appears to be grey. They can also be black, brown or bay. Connemaras stand 13 to 14 h.h., the smaller ones being considered truer to type. The best specimens, in fact, are still bred on the poor, rough pastures that have been their home for so long. Given better conditions—a more equable climate and richer pastures—they begin to lose their inherent pony characteristics.

The Hackney Pony

Not one of the native breeds, the Hackney Pony is nevertheless an important pony breed that originated in Britain. It was developed in the late nineteenth century by a breeder in Westmoreland using a small Yorkshire-bred Hackney stallion. Although it is in effect a smaller version of the Hackney (see page 25) it was developed as a separate and distinctive type and has the essential pony characteristics of a small head carried high, and a compact body. It stands between 12.2 and 14.2

h.h., and possesses the same extravagant high-stepping action of its larger relative, as well as the same gay tail carriage.

Ponies of the USA and South America

The pony of the Americas

This is one of the newest of all breeds, its beginnings dating back little more than twenty years. In 1956, a horse breeder in Iowa crossed a Shetland stallion with an Appaloosa mare. The resulting colt, which in effect was a miniature Appaloosa, was so much admired that it became the founder of a new breed.

Now there is a stud book for the Pony of the Americas. To be eligible for registration, a pony must stand between 11.2 and 13 h.h. and bear one of the six recognized Appaloosa coat patterns (see page 21). For the rest, it is characterized by its fine, Arab-type head, well-arched neck and compact muscular, pony-type body. Like the Appaloosa horses, it has vertically striped hooves. Well over 12,000 ponies are registered now and the breed is extremely popular as a children's riding pony.

The American Shetland

The American Shetland is rather more refined and lighter in appearance, and generally a little taller than its ancestor, the native Shetland ponies of the British Isles. The USA counterpart was developed by controlled breeding from carefully selected ponies imported from Great Britain. It retains the same abundant growth of mane and tail, but generally has a finer coat and rather more exaggerated showy action. It possesses the immense strength of the native breed, as it often demonstrates in weight-pulling contests. It is also required to race in trotting races as well as perform in harness classes, and is of course, popular as a children's riding pony.

The Chincoteague and Assateague

The origin of these ponies, that live mainly on Assateague, an island off the coast of Virginia and Maryland, is uncertain and beset with romantic legend. The story goes that they are descended from Moorish ponies that were being taken by Spanish merchants to Peru to be traded for gold, but which were shipwrecked close to the islands. The ponies apparently swam ashore, thereafter to live and breed, undisturbed and undiscovered for some time, on Assateague. This island they still share only with other wild creatures.

Resembling a small horse rather than a pony in build, they stand about 12 h.h. and although they may be any colour, skewbald and piebald are the most common. Once a year they are rounded up and swum across the narrow channel that separates the two islands, to Chincoteague where they are sold by auction.

The Falabella

This is reputedly the smallest breed of horse in the world, and stands no more than 7 h.h. It was developed in Argentina on a ranch near Buenos Aires owned by the Falabella family. Strangely enough, although the breed has been in existence for less than a hundred years, records of its early development were not kept, so its precise original breeding is not known. However, it is certain that it was developed using Shetland ponies, and thereafter, breeding consistently from the smallest offspring. The aim of the Falabella family was apparently to produce a very small pony with good conformation and a pleasant, tractable nature. Although used as a child's first pony on occasions, it is really more suited to being kept as a pet, and is also popular as a tiny harness pony. Falabellas come in all colours, but the serious breeders of today are tending to concentrate more and more on producing those with Appaloosa markings, as these have become increasingly popular.

Opposite: An American Shetland demonstrates perfectly the taller, considerably lighter build than that of its British Isles cousin and ancestor. American Shetlands are often trained in artificial gaits.

Opposite, inset: The smallest pony in the world, the Falabella. This one has leopard markings.

Below: This Pony of the Americas also displays Appaloosa markings, which are, in fact, a characteristic of the breed. Other characteristics seen here are its short muscular back and rounded barrel.

Ponies of France, Germany and Austria

The Camargue

The Camargue is the best known of France's indigenous ponies. This is the grey pony that shares its watery habitat in the Rhône delta with the equally famous black bulls of the area. The Camargue pony is an old breed, apparently descended from prehistoric horses, but with later infusions of Barb and Arab blood. Surprisingly, it was only officially recognized as a breed in 1967, at which time a breeders' association was formed and the ponies came under the control of the State Stud Administration. They mostly still live in semiwild herds, finding a meagre living on the poor, marshy pastures of the somewhat inhospitable terrain. As with all ponies living under such conditions, they are tough and hardy, sure-footed and full of stamina and able to survive on very frugal rations. Camargue ponies stand up to 14 h.h. and have a rather heavy head, a straight neck tending towards thickness, and a short, strong body. They almost invariably have a huge grass-blown stomach.

The Dülmen

This is one of Germany's two native breeds of pony, but the other, the Senner, is now thought to be extinct. The Dülmen, too, exists in vastly decreased numbers from those it once enjoyed. There would appear to be only one semi-wild herd, kept on a wooded estate in Westphalia. These ponies belong to the Duke of Croy. Crossing with Polish, Welsh Mountain and Arab stallions in recent times means that these ponies are not pure-bred Dülmens, however.

The Dülmen breed has existed for over 600 years and was apparently instrumental in founding, or influencing, the Hanoverian Horse. The ponies stand under 13 h.h. and may be any colour, although black, brown and dun are the most common. Many of the dun-coloured ponies have the black dorsal

Opposite, top: Camargue ponies splash through one of the streams of their wet and marshy habitat.

Opposite, bottom: Dülmen ponies trot through their wooded homeland on the Meerfelder Bruch in W. Germany.

Below: A beautiful example of a Haflinger pony. Pure-bred Haflingers are branded with a symbol of an 'H' incorporated into an edelweiss flower.

or eel stripe down their backs and the zebra markings on their legs, which generally indicate an ancient ancestry. They also frequently appear to be knock-kneed, but this does not seem to affect their movement, which is energetic in all gaits. In addition, they are renowned for their good jumping ability.

The Haflinger

The native pony of the south Tyrol, the Haflinger, is popular and extensively bred in a number of countries besides Austria. Although the breed has ancient origins, all Haflingers in Austria today are said to be able to trace their pedigrees back to a chestnut stallion foaled in the late nineteenth century. He was the result of a crossing between an Arab stallion and a Tirol Haflinger mare. Haflingers are particularly noted for their longevity and it is apparently not unusual to find them still hale and hearty and hard at work as they approach forty years old. They are bred and reared on the lush mountain pastures and generally left there until they are four years old before being broken. Thereafter they are used as riding ponies as well as for harness, pack and light draught work. Standing about 14 h.h., they are chestnut-coloured with a flaxen mane and tail. Living for centuries on mountain terrain has made

them remarkably nimble and sure-footed and they climb up and down the mountainside like a mountain goat. They are also amazingly strong and sound in the wind.

The government has imposed strict controls in the breeding of Haflingers over the last couple of decades, so that the breed is not only on the increase, it has also improved. Both mares and stallions have to pass rigorous tests before they may be used for breeding.

Ponies of Scandinavia and Iceland

The Gotland

Sweden's native pony comes from the island of Gotland, in the Baltic Sea, from which it takes its name. It is a very ancient breed and there is evidence to suggest that it has run wild on the island since the Stone Age. A herd of them still lives semi-wild in the Forest of Löjsta today.

The Gotland pony remains remarkably pure-bred, and true to type, although in the last century it has had infusions of other blood, notably Oriental and Arab. It is bred on the mainland of Sweden, mainly as a children's riding pony—an occupation to which it is well suited once its stubbornness and somewhat fiery temperament have been mastered. It is also used occasionally for harness racing. The Gotland stands 12 to 12.2 h.h. and is a fairly lightly-built pony with a comparatively long head, long back, strong shoulders and sloping quarters. It has energetic paces and is renowned for its outstanding jumping ability.

The Fjord

This is the best known of all pony breeds found in Scandinavia and is a native of Norway. It is, however, popular throughout the Scandinavian coun-tries, particularly Denmark, as well as finding favour in many other European countries and also in Canada. Like the Gotland pony, its ancestry goes back to prehistoric times, and many experts claim it to be descended from Przewalski's Horse (see page 10). Its characteristic, mousy dun coat colour, with black dorsal stripe, silvery black mane, tail and lower legs, together with its coarse scrubby mane that stands up like a scrubbing brush along its thickly crested neck, are certainly features that are found in Przewalski's Horse.

The Fjord is a heavily built pony, with amazing tractive power, a strong,

Below: A hardy Icelandic pony surveys its barren homeland. These ponies are among the most docile and friendly, as well as hard-working, of all native ponies.

Bottom: Besides its popularity as a child's riding pony, the Gotland pony is also used for trotting races.

60

robust constitution and apparently tireless energy and willingness to work. Such factors have made it invaluable to farmers, particularly in the high mountain areas which are still not easily traversed by motorized transport. The ponies are used both as harness and pack animals and also as sturdy, good weight-carrying animals. Although its inherent good nature and kindly disposition, and its height (it stands 13 to 14.2 h.h.), suggest it would make a good child's riding pony, it is really a little too broad for most children and is better suited to carrying adults.

The Icelandic

The friendly little Iceland ponies are a great favourite in their native land, where they are now widely used for trekking. They have inhabited the country from the time it was first invaded and settled by Norsemen in the ninth century. These early settlers brought ponies with them from Norway, carrying them in the traditional Viking long boats on a rough sea voyage that must have taken several days. That the ponies survived such an ordeal gives an indication of their amazing toughness and endurance, traits that are still present in the Icelandic pony today. Besides the Norwegian ponies (which would have resembled the Fjord—see above), other types of pony were brought from the Norse colonies in Scotland and its outlying islands, and to a lesser extent, from Ireland. All these would have interbred to produce the Icelandic pony as we know it today.

It is one of the toughest of all breeds, used to living semi-wild and scratching a meagre living. In the winter, the fish heads thrown to it by the fishermen often comprised its principal food. It stands 12 to 13 h.h. and is most commonly grey or dun-coloured. It has a large head, with a concave profile, a short, thick neck and a short, stocky body. It is reputed to have very good eyesight and also possesses an amazing homing instinct, which makes it very useful for trekkers who lose their way! In addition to the usual walk, trot and canter paces, the Icelandic pony also has an ambling gait, which is comfortable and very safe and steady when covering difficult, rocky or icy terrain. Besides making good riding ponies, capable of carrying people that look far too big for them, the ponies have long been used as pack and harness

animals. In addition, they are sometimes bred especially for meat as beef cattle are unable to survive the harsh Icelandic winters.

Top: The extremely muscular and powerful body and short, thick neck of the Fjord pony are well illustrated here.

Left: A Fjord pony. Note the characteristic mane; a central ridge of black hairs is flanked on either side by a line of silver ones.